T0098565

Do I Need a Divorce to Be Happy?

Advance Praise

"There are a lot of self-help books on the market that make lasting change seem easy. Teri Grayner's book is a breath of fresh air because it is very different. This book asks us to perform an honest assessment of our "stuckness" and how we can – and indeed, must – create authenticity and lasting change in order to live in alignment with our deepest values and truths. Grayner's system, appropriately named REINVENTED, leads us through a process that helps us take responsibility for, and move past, the obstacles that have held us hostage. Part inspirational story and part workbook, this succinct little book is well worth a read. It allows us to see that there is a path out of codependency; Grayner walks alongside us every step of the way."

– Charlotte Chandler Stone,
C-IAYT, E-RYT500
Founder & Director,
Stone Yoga Center for Yoga & Health

"Very well written book with truth and authenticity. I believe that's what the 10 Step REINVENTED process is all about. Teri breaks down the process to teach people how to help themselves. This is not a book about one philosophy to help yourself, but a process that offers you an opportunity to explore ways to look and at yourself and help yourself using real life experience. It really makes the reader think about their decisions on how they live their life and what their goals are for the future.
Very well written and a must read for all to read. Makes you think!"

– Heather Delaney, MSW, LCSW,
LCADC

"Teri Grayner tackles a tough question that many women who lost their sense of freedom and financial independence in their marriage struggle with today. She provides steps that challenge you to develop self-awareness and make choices to reinvent yourself into being the best version of you. She instills hope for overcoming obstacles and reconnecting the relationship to where divorce does not have to be an option."

– Angelia Dickens, PhD, LPC, LMFT, NCC, ACS

"The writer takes the time to explain that while looking into ourselves can be painful, it merits honoring the process. The 10 Step REINVENTED Process breaks down this challenging process, which makes returning to the true self with coping skills possible. One does not need to fall prey to the limited and lacking description of the self that leads to emotional addiction."

– Reverend Craig M. Harris
Author of *LIFE, Living in Fantastic Energy*

"This book is very well written and inspirational. Teri Grayner provides step-by-step guidance for anyone seeking change and growth. I highly recommend this new book."

– Phil Feldman, PhD
Author, *The Psychotherapy Manual*
Adjunct Professor, Rutgers University

"This is an awesome resource to guide you on your journey to a better you. A journey of inspection and reflection and a reminder that all things are possible if you just have the willpower to press forward. Practicing principles in all areas of our lives."

– Dawn Careccio Carpenter

"This book tells the story of a woman that in the midst of challenges learned how to become decisive and overcome incredible odds. It is a must read as she shares how she overcame her traumas and the pitfalls to avoid making your dreams become reality."

– Helen McReynolds, MM, LMT

"My thanks for a very informative tour into the world of codependency, enlightening me into a deeper understanding of a woman's expected role in our society.

A great read for all those who may be able to identify and have a desire to pursue their peace and their self-worth."

— WWW, Bluffton, South Carolina

DO I NEED A DIVORCE

To Be

Happy?

Break Free
from Codependency

TERI GRAYNER

NEW YORK

LONDON • NASHVILLE • MELBOURNE • VANCOUVER

Do I Need a Divorce to Be Happy?

Break Free From Codependency

© 2020 Teri Grayner

Published in New York, New York, by Morgan James Publishing in partnership with Difference Press. Morgan James is a trademark of Morgan James, LLC.
www.MorganJamesPublishing.com

ISBN 9781642795035 paperback
ISBN 9781642795042 eBook
ISBN 9781642795370 audiobook
Library of Congress Control Number: 2019902193

Cover & Interior Design by:
Christopher Kirk
www.GFSstudio.com

Morgan James is a proud partner of Habitat for Humanity Peninsula and Greater Williamsburg. Partners in building since 2006.

Get involved today! Visit
MorganJamesPublishing.com/giving-back

Dedication

For my son Corey,
Your trust in me taught me what it takes surrender.
It ultimately transformed me
into showing up as the real me.
Thank you for having the strength to walk
through your fear into your own freedom.
*You are **awesome**!*
To the Morgan James Publishing team: Special
thanks to David Hancock, CEO & Founder for
believing in me and my message. To my Author
Relations Manager, Gayle West, thanks for making
the process seamless and easy. Many more thanks to
everyone else, but especially Jim Howard, Bethany
Marshall, and Nickcole Watkins.

Table of Contents

Introduction

*"Don't let your wishes and dreams die
tugging on your heartstrings…"*

I love you and you love me and I support you
… and then I realize you don't support me!
Sound familiar? What's a girl to do? It's all
really just a matter of perspective and we make
choices and we decide how we want to live life.
Although you do need to honor your God-given
gifts, heartfelt wishes, and dreams, or you stand
to let them die tugging on your heartstrings.

If you are a person who spends the majority of your days doing more for your husband/
partner and family members than for yourself,

read on. If you think about your current circumstances and it stresses you out to think about
making time for your own needs – everything
else seems to take precedence – read on.

You probably don't need to divorce your
partner. You may need to give yourself permission to divorce your current way of thinking. It
may have become outdated, obsolete, and very
difficult to live with any longer. And that is a
great sign because it is only the beginning to
having a better life for yourself.

Marriage doesn't mean you have to sacri-
fice yourself for your partnership. But what I
am asking you is to consider is what happens if
either partner at some point in their life journey
together does not feel that they have what they
need for their own happiness. Would it shake
the marriage to the core? And would it impact
its future?

Let's face it, marriage is a partnership
and working together is essential for success,
but the individuals in the partnership need
to feel that they are living in their own per-

sonal strength to sustain the ups and downs of working together.

So, now we have identified that it is difficult to continue serving goals and dreams that don't fit into your current mindset. If you ask me, it is very difficult for your mind and body to tolerate living in a conflicted state. And the end result is eventually one or the other wins out. Don't get me wrong, people are not going to always be transparent, but how does realistic sound? How can problems be solved together? Better yet, I ask you can your goals be achieved without integrity?

I am sure if you think about it, there are many examples you can draw from where you have seen people trying to live outside of their integrity and then what do you witness? Their status quo catches up with their truth and we know they are not living in alignment and then one day *BAM!* They have a crisis and are forced to make a change. Nobody likes it when these things happen because it usually results in a cat-astrophic situation, but the reality is that it happens. And while it looks like it is the worst thing that could have happened, in the end it turns out to be the best for everyone involved.

Seriously though, I am not kidding when I say that your dreams and goals die tugging on your heart strings if you do not address them – the reality is that they do. It is much more difficult to accept these facts when they become a painful reality, but why wait until that happens? It takes less energy to address the problem than the effort it will take to protect and defend a mindset that is no longer true.

I'll bet there has been something very stable and consistent in your life. Yes, and it probably looks like security, especially if you don't rock the boat too much. You may have a regular full time job that does not demand much, but it pays the bills. Your husband is considered the primary breadwinner of the family and life looks like they told you it would look when you became an adult. This consistency is not something to take lightly or dismiss just because it is how our lives make sense and to some extent it is our reality. If you think there is something else you need to be doing there probably is and I am sure these thoughts are keeping you from falling asleep at night. However, if you find that you are waking up in the middle of the night questioning your current situation it's because deep down you really desire change but are not sure what the first step is, then we need to talk.

Let's be practical here, it may be worth taking a closer look at your life and being a little more honest with yourself about what you truly feel is working for you and what is not. It is overwhelming to take this approach, but if you know deep down inside that you are you are not feeling good about your life in its current state, what's the worst that could come out of taking a realistic look at the situation?

Isn't it worth making the changes you desire to see your dreams become your reality? Your dreams and goals are worth your time and attention and they can be accomplished. The question I have for you is can you see yourself achieving your goals and dreams in the next five years if you made the changes you needed to get there? If your answer is a resounding yes, even if it isn't exactly five years, then read on. Generally, planning for the future is measured in five year increments. If you do not have a vision for your future with an estimated timetable for achieving your goals, you may not be in the mindset this book is planning on taking you toward; however, that's okay. Please enjoy reading on to see if that remains true.

When you open your heart to these questions, it is most likely that your heart has been trying to tell you something for a long time and this is not a coincidence. *Please do not ignore these questions at this point because failure to address them will only result in increased stress and they have the power to create collateral damage if they are not addressed.*

Here is what my experience has taught me: your heart has been trying to get your attention and if it wasn't, you would not have picked up this book. Most people talk to their friends and family about their hopes and dreams. Usually what they get back is one of a few things. Friends will agree with your desire for change and then reinforce your current situation, stating that your life is very stable and consistent, certainly better than most. Your family will entertain your thoughts and share their hopes and dreams, but reinforce that you have the majority of what you want in life and your needs are being met so why rock the boat.

I speak about my process on the *Psychology Today* website as a therapist. I teach my process to my clients and patients and have mentored many individuals in the helping field. While I believe wholeheartedly in my process, I must inform you that I have reinvented my life many times and found the secret ingredient for success.

So I developed a ten-step process called R.E.I.N.V.E.N.T.E.D. I refer to the process in the past tense so when you are following the process your mindset is geared toward accomplishing your goals instead of mentally creating barriers to why your goals cannot be achieved.

My process is very straightforward and may come across at first as too good to be true because it's so simple. However, it will take a commitment on your part and conscious effort to make the change you want to see in your life.

R – Reason for change.

It's important to identify your reason for the change you want to make in your life. You need to be in a state of mind where deep down inside you know you are ready and when you see the signs that the vehicle has shown up to get you that you are prepared to go forward.

E – Eliminate excuses.

Eliminate the excuses that hold you back from taking action toward making your dreams your reality. Be prepared to do the inside work that it will take to prepare yourself to implement the change you want to make. Building confidence.

I – Identify your voice.

It's about getting really clear on who you are and what you feel you need to set your goals into motion.

N – Normalize change.

Focus on incorporating the process you are taught here into your daily routine. Working toward your goals means that you are willing to work through the inconvenience of meditation and journaling daily until you are doing it automatically.

V – Visualize achieving your goals.

It's about getting all of your senses involved in the awareness of what you want to achieve.

E- Expand your vision.

Have basic goals and dreams to expand on and expect your vision to change over time.

N – Nurture your vision.

Make time to create a vision board with words, pictures, drawings of what you want to create in your life,

T – Take time

Allow yourself to take the time you need to grow your goals and dreams into what ultimately drives you to achieve your goals. Be willing to do the physically uncomfortable things it takes to grow into the new version of yourself.

E – Embrace freedom.

Embrace the opportunity to create what you want your life to become. Mentally exercise your thoughts by creating visual tools to see the end product in mind.

D – Detach with love.

Detach yourself from your expectations and the expectations of others. Allow yourself to be led instead of doing the leading. Experience what it feels like to let go of control of the outcome.

The ten-step REINVENTED process will offer you hope when you feel like giving up and it will remind you that if you did not have what it takes to make the changes in your life you would not still be reading this chapter. Smile! I will show you the decision-making process and you will see how it naturally flows when you connect to what your heart has been trying to tell you.

Some strategies in this book will sound practical and mainstream, which may make you feel inclined to follow that specific path. Invariably this will seem to make the most sense and appear to be the clear and direct path to breaking the barriers to becoming financially independent *while not breaking your marriage.* It will draw you in as the obvious direct path to success. Upon further investigation, most people find that this is what we call the path of least resistance. In the beginning of this journey, it will be appealing and have you tempted to tell your friends and family that you have made a commitment to get counseling. But don't do it. Why? That will be explained to you as you read a little further. However, when we are ready to make a change in our lives we want to see evidence that it is happening right away. And it is a sign of enthusiasm, but part of the process is learning to have patience with yourself so your efforts will serve you for the long haul. Other aspects of being in a hurry are described as impulsive behaviors because behind them are actions that throw a red flag that your decisions are being made with your head and not your heart. This book will also cover the pitfalls you will learn to avoid in your decision-making process.

Chapter 1:

The Answer Is....

This story might feel familiar to you. Melissa is a 34-year-old senior accountant who was raised in an upper middle-class town in Bergen County, New Jersey. She currently resides with her husband and three children in a town nearby. Her husband of eighteen years is an accountant who spends a majority of his time away from the home working and traveling for business. Melissa is currently on maternity leave as she has just given birth to their third child.

When we spoke last, she told me the early years of their marriage were exciting, as their careers were taking off and they successfully saved to buy their first home. Shortly after, they were established in their new home, their first child was born. And their second child came along two years later. Now the first two children are in high school. While Melissa thought the days of waking up in the middle of the night to tend to babies crying were over, she found herself announcing the birth of their third child into the world. While babies are a miracle, this was a life-altering change for Melissa. She now found herself consumed with thoughts that had her feeling differently about her life and she was unclear how to express what all of that meant. She did find herself preoccupied with these thoughts as she tried to fall asleep at night.

Since she did not have the luxury to be a stay-at-home mom in the past, she was now feeling that this would be a dream come true. She was now entertaining the idea for real. So, before she discussed it with her husband John, she decided to phone her lifetime dear friend and counsel.

First, I received a text message from her saying that she needed a minute of my time to sort through a few thoughts that had been waking her up in the middle of the night. She told me that she didn't need my advice as much as she needed a sounding board to sort out her thoughts. The clue here was that Melissa had a life-altering situation and it prompted her to make changes in her life.

We spoke at length later on that evening and she told me that these thoughts had been haunting her for years and that she did not pay much attention to them because she had committed to the goals she had set with her husband, John, when they were caught up in the excitement of marriage, careers, and buying a home together. And now she said that she wanted to talk to John about her goals, but she was afraid that he would not make the time to listen to her thoughts and dreams or he would dismiss what she had to say altogether because they had been putting all their energy into their retirement goals. Thankfully, she knew she needed a support system to get through this part of her problem.

So, I asked her ideally what she wanted to see happen and if that would ultimately be a "dream come true." Now I know a dream come true can sound idealistic at first but remember this is about Melissa creating her ideal situation.

So, I worked with Melissa to get her to open up about her fears and the thoughts that were keeping her up at night. Then I asked her if there was no fear involved, what would she ultimately be wanting to see change in her current circumstances and how she would want John to support her to have what she really wanted. Initially she had trouble putting her answer into words especially since she was projecting in her mind how John was going to react to this sudden change in their plans. Then I said, "Melissa, what is it costing you to not address this problem? In other words, how is the stress of not addressing this situation impacting you personally?" I asked her to think about the questions I had asked her and told her that we would talk again the following day.

When we spoke again the following day, since Melissa had gotten the urgency off her back to speak she recoiled and said to me, "Well," and then she sighed and said, "I feel guilty thinking about what I want to do for myself." And she followed that thought by saying, "John has been focused on the retirement plan we established early on in our marriage. We review it every five years and the thought of telling John that I want to invest in a career change instead of our retirement plan will make him angry and could cause a fight. I don't like tension in our relationship." Melissa needed to review her self-value.

She started to pull away from our conversation, making excuses that she was overwhelmed when she thought about telling John how she was really feeling and that she was mentally and physically exhausted. This was more than about losing interest in their original goals and dreams. Melissa had spent too many years procrastinating and daydreaming about approaching John about his lack of support for her goals and dreams and expressing to him how that made her feel. I validated Melissa's feelings about living with a lack of passion and now having a new baby on top of it all was too much for anyone to experience. Then I reminded her that there are consequences to holding space for an old belief system when you are no longer committed to it because it is like trying to live a double life and eventually something has to give. Right now Melissa was experiencing unnecessary pressure on her mind, body, and spirit. She did not tell me, but I could feel that she was coming to a breaking point. I could hear this in her voice when she spoke to me, but when she was around John she put on her happy face to not only keep him happy but to hold onto that feeling of security, being emotionally attached to him and their financial arrangement. She totally agreed with me and said she was recently feeling more mentally and physically drained by acting like everything was fine to keep her relationship with John from falling apart.

This is not new. Melissa was suffering from many unaddressed problems from the past and now she was feeling that she was feeling the pressure of her marital issues. Her sigh was acknowledgement that the weight of carrying these problems was becoming more of a burden to carry. She knew that her situation was complex, but it was resolvable if she only could get the time to talk to John. She knew that she would feel so much better if she could talk to John, but she was so used to putting herself last that she could not imagine what it would be like to put herself first. Besides, John would never have it that way and she knew that. However, she felt the only solution to her problem was to find a way to lighten the load before she lost everything, so she made a decision to put herself first and begin to follow the REINVENTED process. Now it was time for her to take action.

I was concerned about how long Melissa had been avoiding counseling, so my concern was that she already had known for a long time what not solving this problem was costing her.

Don't forget, Melissa was very intelligent and a master at solving everyone else's problems, but over the years had grown so attached to John and the goals and dreams they set together that her stomach sank even thinking about bringing the topic up.

Keeping that in mind, if the tables were turned and her husband told her he needed her support to make changes in their retirement plans so that he could work on a new career path, she would be all in. She would rise to the occasion and be the supportive wife that she's always been and help him to achieve his goals and dreams. However, now that this situation was about her, it was more complicated because she was a people pleaser.

At this point, Melissa did not have to have all the pieces of the puzzle figured out, but the one thing she needed to decide was if she was sick and tired of being sick and tired. She did say that she was mentally and physically drained thinking about continuing with their established retirement goals. She knew that the baby was a wakeup call for her to make a major change in her life only the baby was the only wakeup call she addressed.

That is the primary focus of this book. I am not only a number one bestselling author, but counselor who speaks from twenty years of experience – not exclusively from clinical interventions, but also from life experiences. Before we move on, let's review Melissa's dilemma.

She had woken up to the fact that she couldn't continue to live the way she had been living and felt she must change her life direction. The first step for her to take was to get herself into counseling, to begin to write down her thoughts, her wishes, her hopes, and her dreams. Basically anything that kept her connected to the feeling of solving her problem.

In this book, we will discuss actions to take and pitfalls to avoid so that you can keep your focus. You will learn how to bring clarity to your ideas and focus to making your own dreams come true. I will teach you the benefit of taking time to sort out your ideas from your thoughts to avoid confusion. The primary goal is to work through the obstacles that keep you from having the confidence to make your dreams come true.

Chapter 2:

Do You Identify?

If the definition of insanity is doing the same thing over and over expecting different results. Nothing is more true. In fact, there is no evidence to prove this statement is false.

Let's review what has been happening to Melissa. She told me that she has spent her life being a people pleaser. I know that can sound like a good thing especially if you identify with how good it makes you feel to "help others." But at what point does it become a detriment to you? I am speaking about the disease of codependency.

My point being that when our lives revolve around another person's expectations of us our spirit starts to fade into the background. We lose ourselves. We become so invested in another person's ideas and dreams, we become emotionally invested, enmeshed into the other person's emotions, and then it becomes difficult to separate your thoughts, feelings, and emotions from theirs. This situation creates a high level of expectations and holds more space for increased pain and emotional wounds.

There are many ways to define codependency, so I am only trying to give you traits of the disease. Melissa was suffering from financial codependency. She had in fact bound herself to John by being co-dependent as she said she was afraid to approach him about ideas she had for change but she had also muted her voice by allowing his actions to dominate her decisions.

I will expand on what codependency looks like and how it is developed. First, it is an unhealthy emotional attachment to a person, place, or thing. In early childhood we form a natural emotional attachment to our caregivers. But what if our primary caregiver is unhealthy?

This makes them emotionally unavailable. Let's say for example, they have a mental illness, alcoholism, or an addiction? It rarely matters what they are preoccupied with; the problem is just the mere fact that they are preoccupied with something outside of themselves and cannot give of themselves what they don't have. Are you beginning to understand the process?

So, codependency is defined as a disease because we are reacting to an illness. The illness can be identified as a compulsive disorder such as alcoholism or addiction. These illnesses are progressive in nature and they increase with intensity over time.

Lastly, there are twelve-step recovery groups available to address these issues, one being CoDa. CoDa is built on the following principles of honesty, hope, faith, courage, integrity, willingness, humility, brotherly/sisterly love, justice, perseverance, spiritual awareness, and service work. They are the same principles of AA, NA, and all of the other twelve-step programs in existence today.

Now back to your opportunity to make change in your life. You can add a morning routine to your daily routine, if you do not have one already established. You start to incorporate actions into your morning routine that turn your focus inward.

And it is likely to look like change, but it may bear too much resemblance to your current circumstances, offering a minimally improved sense of satisfaction. It is only the familiar that is surfacing.

It may bring up uncomfortable feelings and a sense of dis-ease. Don't stop when this happens. The past will surface at the attempt to grab your attention and steal your focus. It is only thoughts and feeling that have been sitting dormant and unaddressed inside you for so long. Over time, they become so familiar that we overlook their presence. I will show you how to manage uncomfortable feelings in the REIN-VENTED process.

If your heart is calling you to take action and you are searching for something that will make your heart sing. If you are nodding your head in agreement while you are reading this paragraph, this is good. Now read on.

Consider this. It is natural to follow what is comfortable, as I've mentioned before, but isn't it more natural to follow your heart? I challenge you to take some time to look back at the hopes and dreams you had for yourself before you may have chosen to move them lower on your list of priorities.

So, why be different? Give yourself a moment to reflect on this answer and jot down thoughts and feelings that come to mind. Write down your answer and be as detailed as you can. If you don't know that answer, then ask yourself the following questions: "What is the payoff for remaining the same?" "What am I gaining if I keep things the same?" These are key questions to moving forward with your goals and dreams.

Do you remember coming across this inspirational statement by Marianne Deborah Williamson? It sounds something like this: "Our deepest fear is not that we are inadequate. Our deepest fear is that we are powerful beyond measure. It is our light not our darkness that frightens us. Your playing small does not serve the world, etc." Well, this is the message that will be your new inspiration: *Don't let your goals and dreams die tugging on your heart strings.* And when the timing is right you will compare your past to where you want to be in the future and set your goals to get there.

Acceptance that our dreams are not the same as they once were can make you feel an ache in the pit of your stomach that speaks to your soul, reminding you that you have been on the wrong path for quite some time. Don't turn your back on yourself here. What I want you to consider is, if you were able to move out of your current situation, what would make you think it would be a wise decision to return to the familiar as uncomfortable as it remains at this time? Could you see yourself tolerating that sinking feeling in the pit of your stomach for much longer?

Right now, it is more important to identify what you need to do for you. The fact is that sometimes we have to face the reality that our partner may be more consumed in serving themselves by overworking or by being overly focused on retirement and that may not include making you their number one priority.

Sometimes we bring our goals and dreams to our partner for support and find that they are not supportive of us. That can create hurt feelings and feeling a loss from their lack of support and make us feel crushed. After the hurt subsides, negative feelings start to grow toward the other person because we recognize them as "the one" who does not support our goals and dreams. It is difficult to come to terms with resenting another person, especially if you are married to them.

Regardless of how our circumstances can create resentments and cause us to react toward others unjustly. This can and will take us completely off of focusing on ourselves and our goals and dreams. It would not be a wise choice to take positive energy that can be applied toward your goals and turn it into negative energy focusing on the grudge you feel toward your partner for not being supportive.

If we decide to focus on the negative energy, it becomes misdirected anger, which is mentally maintained by thoughts reinforcing it as justifiable anger. When we are ready to face the enemy in the mirror, it usually is that moment when it cannot be put off any longer. At last, the time comes to let go of all of the wasted energy being invested in negative feelings.

When emotional responses become reactive responses and increasingly become blown out of proportion and difficult to manage over time while making you feel sick to your stomach, this is the active disease of codependency. It is obviously an emotional disorder; however, emotional disorders manifest in the body as chronic aches and pains. The fact is that while the mind plays tricks on us, the body tells us otherwise. Just like our heartstrings pull on us and send a signal to the brain that something is wrong, the tightness in our stomachs, the cramps in our hips, and the tension in our thighs are doing the same thing. They are trying to get our attention.

Our minds may tell us we can fight past the emotional bonds as we try to break free from others, but we usually return to the scene of the crime to fix the brokenness of our original relationships through the new relationships we form. Feelings of hopelessness, isolation, depression, emotional or physical illness, and potentially suicidal fantasies come up to the surface to rear their ugly heads once again.

We are a self-destructive, relationship-poor people remaining in sickness until one day the light goes on in our heads and we awaken to the possibility of having more and strive to heal ourselves and break free of our codependency.

Unfortunately, sometimes before we arrive at the motivation to get treatment for this deadly disease, the dis-ease in the body manifests itself into a chronic illness, a long list of health issues, or a life-threatening illness. The dis-ease of body, mind, and spirit manifests evidence and it is called illness.

We are literally immersed and embodied in emotional pain and unresolved grief and don't know where to begin to resolve. As dreams die, so does a part of our soul. The illness can have an impact on all areas of our lives as well. Our children are most affected, then our extended family and friends. Emotional pain and unresolved grief like the disease of alcoholism can dissolve income, relationships, social life, and even material wealth.

Tell me, what is not solving your problem costing you? What are you willing to let it cost you? Please don't tell me you are willing to live your entire life without challenging your fears. What is your desire? Do you realize your heart's desire's waiting for you to solve this problem and it will continue to wait?

Chapter 3:

What to Expect

This book is in your hands right now because you want to make changes in your life circumstances and you have unresolved questions that are simply questions that you have chosen to not address with yourself yet.

Once you make the decision that it is time to change your life direction you will never have to ask another person for permission. The answers to your problems will start to unfold.

Deciding to make the time to find clarity and peace of mind for yourself tells the universe you are ready to receive something better.

The choices you have made have gotten you to this point in your life. And now you will see what a change in your perspective brings your way.

I suggest you begin with the practice of meditation. Being open yourself to a new way of thinking and learning is the first step. Remember to be gentle with yourself learning a brand-new way of living. Start by focusing your mind on your breath. Now, bring yourself to the awareness of your breath as it flows in and out of your body. Observe your breathing pattern and notice what it is like when you are stressed. Clear your thoughts and refocus on your breath and you will see how you have calmed your breath with clearing your mind. Now you are on the road to wellness and recovery.

You will become more aware of your breathing pattern and recognize when you sigh that you are stressed. You can put this into practice by beginning in this moment. Place this book on your lap and take a moment to focus on your breathing pattern. Then pause and redirect your mind to intentionally inhale and pause for a second and then exhale. Notice how the muscles in your chest and shoulders shift while you are filling your lungs. The is the beginning of learning how to engage in the self-care practice of meditation.

Practicing meditation will increase the blood flow to the brain and release endorphins to reduce stress when you need to get your mind clear and refocus. An alternative meditation technique is progressive muscle relaxation. It is an excellent way to prepare for a good night's sleep. It helps to clear your thoughts and allows your mind to rest and refresh itself for the new day ahead.

Meditation can also be done while you are taking a walk, simply by focusing your mind on the deliberate action of walking. This is referred to as a mindfulness technique when you allow yourself to focus on the steps you are taking, the fresh air you are breathing into your lungs, and the wind as it gently brushes your face when you are walking.

Another skillset I recommend developing for personal growth is journaling. It can begin with the habit of writing down your thoughts or feelings. Journaling is a positive habit that is worth developing. Not just because it can be a good resource to refer to when you are sorting out your thoughts and feelings, but because it is cathartic and healing on every level, mentally, emotionally, and spiritually. It clears your mind and that is only one healing byproduct.

First, when you write down your thoughts, it creates space for your brain for improve concentration and to focus. Secondly, you don't lose the value of thoughts and ideas because you are able to put them in a safe place to meditate on at a later time. You will be increasing your self-esteem by practicing the habit of valuing your thoughts and feelings.

Journaling is the gateway to your freedom. After you develop a regular habit of journaling, new ideas will come through more readily and inspiration will flow through you with more grace and ease.

It is a habit that is not only a coping skill, but a self-soothing tool because you hold the space for your thoughts and feelings. I am sure you have experienced speaking to a friend seeking feedback on an idea and found that they may not have understood you the way you had hoped. In contrast, you may have found turning your attention to your own thoughts and feelings you obtained a sense of satisfaction like no other. This is a form of self-care and a very important one at that.

Journaling brings us closer to ourselves and to our feelings and will help you start to notice moments when you feel a sense of revelation and connection to thoughts and ideas that you thought were long gone. When we don't write, we lose that connection to what fulfills us, and when we consistently write, we build on our thoughts and ideas and open our hearts. It brings clarity to thought and empowers our feelings because they get a voice.

In the same respect, when we release what is trapped in our mind it stands to reason that unacknowledged thoughts, feelings, and ideas will flow through you onto the pages of your journal and you can read them back for further exploration. Don't be surprised if your journaling doesn't make any sense to you when you read it back, because this is a tool that can also be used to unlock parts of ourselves that may have been closed up for a long time. Be patient with yourself and the process of discovery. Ultimately, you will recognize your thoughts and ideas and they will make perfectly good sense to you.

You will begin to recognize that the things you wanted for yourself were inside you somewhere because other things in life seemed so much more important. Getting yourself connected to a professional counselor who has good working knowledge of twelve-step recovery is going to help you dive a little deeper into your self-discovery and ultimately help you to reveal to yourself your long-lost goals and dreams. Developing the practice of self-care by experiment with journaling will help you accelerate your path of self-discovery. You will find that you are living more with a happier mindset and you may also find that you are sleeping better and feeling more refreshed in the morning. If you are an early riser, you may also enjoy the benefits of journaling in the morning. Your mind is still in an unconscious state, giving you access to unconscious thoughts. Be willing to experiment with the process by sitting quietly after getting out of bed and write down what you experience.

Consequently, personal growth takes place on many levels. Here is another exercise I suggest for you to try. It is a known fact that when you identify and write down three things you are grateful for and why you feel that way before going to sleep, it creates a rippling effect in your subconscious mind while you sleep. You are initiating the practice of programming your subconscious mind to seek out more positive experiences and reasons to be grateful, even initiating experiences that bring you gratitude.

There is value in developing the practice of gratitude. I suggest you try taking a thirty-day challenge of writing down three things you are grateful for every evening before you fall asleep and see if you notice positive changes developing in your life.

Gratitude is a positive thought process and when we focus on it, it sends a message of appreciation. Positive thoughts are energy and have a specific vibration translating into feelings of gratitude or joy.

When our energy vibrates in the state of joy, everything around us is a recipient of the energy of pure joy. Joy is the most beautiful energy there is on this planet next to love. Love is all there is and there is no more. We all know the power of love, self-love, and pure love energy. It heals all that is receptive to receiving its energy. You have heard the expression that "love heals all," and it is true.

Happiness is a choice and you are holding the key to it in your hands right now. I challenge you to take a moment to consider what your life will look like five years down the road if you continue to make the same choices. Do you see your life looking more like you dreamed? Or does the thought of your life continuing on the same path make you feel a dull pain in the pit of your stomach?

My suggestion to you then is to continue to read on and see if the dull pain in your stomach turns into a sudden increase in your pulse and an increased heart rate that feels like a sudden burst of excitement that has been reborn from a distant memory being reignited.

Chapter 4:

Melissa's Story

Just to catch you up on what went on with Melissa after she told me about her sleepless nights: she did continue to wrestle with conflicting thoughts running through her mind. She began the practice of morning meditations and journaling at night and even jotting down her thoughts during the day when they came to her.

Then one day it became apparent to her that she was really just tired of lying to herself. She asked herself many times if she should continue to hide these feelings and thoughts that she was no longer happy with their long-term retirement plan from John.

She knew that John would not be happy, so she decided to go to counseling to work through her own personal struggles with her individuality. Melissa had a difficult childhood and brought a lot of baggage into her relationship with John, so over time it became more difficult to identify if John was the problem or if how she perceived her situation was the real problem.

After six months in counseling she discovered that she had a lump on her breast. She knew that now she had to see her primary care doctor to possibly initiate a series of doctor's visits to take care of herself. It was evident to her that she had stuffed her feelings for too long. Imagine the things she began to discover when she attended her regular counseling sessions.

Melissa, who appeared to be meek to some and a pushover to others, had now gone from being a part of everyone else's life to putting herself first in her own life.

She returned to work and put the baby in daycare because she knew it was what needed to be done. There was no turning back and she couldn't look at John to blame him for being overly focused on work and their retirement plan. He had worked hard and deserved to keep their plans on track. But what he did not see coming was Melissa's illness.

If you recall what I had mentioned earlier in the book, that if you continue to hold space for what no longer serves you, the universe will collapse your current plans (since they no longer serve you) and present you with something more complicated.

Well, both John and Melissa had to learn how to work together to get Melissa through her breast cancer diagnosis. John had to hire someone to come into their home and help Melissa with the children and housework. That person stayed longer hours as Melissa progressed with her treatments and additional surgeries.

Melissa and John both realized that if they were going to have each other in their lives for the long term they were going to have to work harder now more than ever. Melissa made time for herself to practice her self-care routines of meditation and journaling while she focused on getting well.

Melissa's family that lived nearby came to visit more frequently and helped with the children on the weekends. Overall, their family grew stronger in the throes of adversity. When John was able to, he would take the children on weekend day trips so Melissa could rest, as the therapies were sometimes difficult for her physically.

She did not realize the impact of not having a consistent self-care daily routine. Her childhood had mentally trained her to be tough, taught her the way to avoid more pain is to fix problems and that in turn distracted her from establishing and keeping self-care routines for herself.

Both of her parents subscribed to that philosophy, as did her grandparents on both sides. It really wasn't her fault. During the next weeks, she attended breast cancer support groups and came across survivors as well as women who saw their illness as a death sentence. This led her to meeting women with late stage cancer, living with treatments that were only prolonging their lives, and saw that their attitude toward life was spiritual.

Melissa continued to have sessions with her counselor on the phone if she was not able to make it physically into her office. She began to have insight into the self-destructive thought patterns she had established and where they had gotten her in life.

One afternoon while Melissa was attending a support group, she met a woman who asked her if she was interested in working a couple of hours a week working with teens who needed to be home schooled.

She eventually went for an interview to begin working as a bedside teacher. She was hired on the spot because of her sincere interest in helping the teens. Melissa was working a few hours a week for about a month when one of her coworkers asked her if she could cover for them running a therapy group that evening at the counseling center.

Now, you do remember that my recommendation was to meditate and journal to connect to your heart and give it a voice, right? Well, it was when Melissa found herself running a group for teens with drug addiction that she realized that all the practice of self-care had brought her to an opportunity that she had given up on obtaining many, many years ago.

You just never know how much self-care can impact your life until you stop fighting the practice and open yourself up to the process of being one with your heart.

Melissa could have gotten there sooner if she had started working with me earlier, but the point is that she got there!

Chapter 5:

My Story....

If you are lying awake at night thinking about your life being everything you have ever wanted and then this little voice interrupts you and says your heart doesn't feel that way, chances are you know it deep down inside too. It may be time to take a closer look at what that voice is trying to say.

It's not easy to look inside yourself and get the answers you seek nor is it easy to see what version of you the world can see. So, I ask you to take a look inside yourself and ask yourself if your life up to this point is something that has been very stable and consistent, where you cannot imagine disturbing the day in and out routine no matter how mundane it feels it is, because one false move would make your "house of cards" collapse. This is a version of the definition of insanity where you do the same thing over and over, but deep down inside you are wishing for different results.

So now, what if you end up really loving your partner and don't even love yourself? Worse … what happens if you realize you don't love your partner and you don't even love yourself? Then what? Your heart is broken in two and you end up having to throw both pieces in the garbage – or worse, waste a lot of time trying to figure out which part you want to mend.

My loyalty is to you, dear one. Hopefully you won't have to take the long way home back to your heart. It is my heartfelt duty to share with you my story in an effort to help you make choices that serve you even if they don't seem like they are the right thing to do at the time. Guilt is a family disease and people enjoy making themselves and each other so sick sometimes that the only thing they can do is get worse instead of better.

I depend on love from you and you depend on love from me. Maybe that isn't what your family preached, but it was what mine made a practice of reinforcing. United we stand and divided we fall. What if one pulls away to be their real selves? Does that mean they don't love their family?

I was raised with the mindset that traditionally, the man goes to go to work every day and come home either happy or mad. He is viewed as the primary breadwinner. So, consequently he makes the financial decisions for the family. The woman's job is viewed as secondary income.

Now it is time to consider what happens if you don't agree with the family model I just described to you. I don't know if I spent one too many lifetimes fighting the message of self-love or what exactly happened, but I was living in one value system and practicing another. I did not agree with my family value system and this motivated me to become strong and independent.

I knew deep down inside I was meant to bring this message to women that it is good to be independent and break free from being bound to a relationship. Don't get me wrong, I believe in love and relationships, but not to the point where it would take my life. Out of all the lessons I learned growing up, I knew my family life would be way different.

Although it took me a long time to realize the value of self-care I eventually did and I brought it into my daily routine because it helps me thrive and live my life instead of just getting by every day. I became a healer because I don't like to see people suffer. I coped with the challenges of healing because there are plenty of them. I just wanted to do what I had to do to live a life with a sense of being whole and having peace of mind. I just could not connect to the true happiness I was seeking for myself.

My life was like that for many years. I was diagnosed with breast cancer. I did recover from it because I was determined to live a life beyond my wildest dreams and I knew that day was coming as long as I was still alive and open to the opportunity.

With all that being said, my life after cancer was packed with every self-help practice known in search of that inner peace I longed for my whole life. I did not know how the answer would present itself to me so I focused on healing my pain. Sad to report I felt after almost twenty years of working on myself I found practices that helped, but nothing that moved my heart like I knew it would when I found it. I was just about to throw in the towel and said to a friend that I felt I just hadn't changed enough to find that true happiness. Just a side note, I will share with you that I had been using a long-standing coping skill I created myself called "the happiness factor." That was my way of dealing with the ups and downs of life and filling in the gaps where there was no immediate solution. It was the habit of identifying things that felt good and if they did I added them to my emotional bank account by making a statement that they were contributing to "the happiness factor."

Now to get back to my story, I am sure you can guess how I decided to handle the obstacle in front of me. If you answered try one more time then you are correct. I had to give it one last ditch effort and I did manifest the opportunity to attend one more self-help workshop. So, I took all the money I had saved for a rainy day and hopped on a plane and flew to Puerto Rico.

I presented my problem as clearly as I could in that moment and I didn't realize it at the time, but I had made the decision to reconnect to my heart and soul. Remember that healing from painful experiences and witnessing other people's pain takes time to heal and mend what was once broken. It has to be done with intention and authenticity. With that, I decided I wanted to align with my soul's purpose and live my authentic life. That is how I spent all my years of learning, being open to being vulnerable to myself while reconnecting all the particles of my soul.

Yet, I needed to continuously work on my own codependency and what's more, I could improve to strengthen myself. After coping so long with challenges, I adopted a survival practice of habits and behaviors and the truth is, if you desire happiness in life it will take a continuous practice to change those habits and behaviors for that to happen. I had to break free from financial codependency too.

You see, you can break bad habits and take back your life in many ways and while most healers are under the misconception that they have worked it all out, remember we are humans, not perfect people. There is no such thing as perfect people, except as portrayed on TV shows and written about in books. It does not make it a fact. It makes it another version of insanity, which is doing the same thing over and over expecting different results.

Our circumstances don't dictate how happy we are; we dictate how happy we are and our circumstances fall into place behind our attitude. I did have to learn how to divorce my own thinking. I had to stop having a lifetime relationship with money and decide to have a real relationship with a people. That practice was initiated by developing a relationship with myself. Without developing that relationship with myself I would have never been able to break free from financial codependency.

The dream I have for anyone reading this book looking for change is to not take the long road to making the change they need to make. My life was filled with suffering internally before I got sick simply because deep down I wanted to feel, but I was terrified of it at the same time, so I chose to complicate the way I looked at my life and its problems.

You can literally turn your life around in eight weeks by building the confidence you need to confront what is standing in your way. You do not have to get a diagnosis of cancer like Melissa did before you decide that it is time to step into action and work on your goals and dreams. *That is just too much work!*

Choose to allow your intuition to guide you. Go with what your gut tells you is right because, remember, your mind can tell you scary stories, but your body will always be the truth barometer.

Use your God-given gifts and the wisdom you were born with to guide you to the counsel and coaching you need and deserve to live the best version of yourself today. Why wait?

The excuses will be waiting for you if you decide you want to put this book down and ignore your truth. Whichever way you decide to perceive your situation, you can and that is always going to be your choice.

This is not the end of my story; it is only the beginning of how I reclaimed my life one moment at a time, one hour at a time, and one day at a time. I continue to do that up until this day and if you stick with me, you can get there easier, faster, in a more organized way learning how to avoid the pitfalls and obstacles along the way.

Chapter 6:

The Process

You may find yourself googling the following: divorce, money and marriage, emotionally trapped, confidence, intimidated, bound, stuck, blocked, looking for a way out, emotionally abused, or codependency. And what have you found as a direct result of your search?

The situation you are currently facing is a crossroad. It is a place of indecision. Staying in the mindset of indecision can lead to an indefinite loss of time where you could have been productive. And what that means is if you know you have to make a change, and you decide to delay taking action, you could find yourself mentally stuck there and it can become extremely painful. You could feel stuck when you fear the pain. Maybe it will take the pain becoming greater than the fear of the pain to move into action.

If you are coming from the mindset of judgement, it is like telling yourself your situation is permanent and unremovable. You might see your situation as irreparable, but that is your choice. The good news is that is your choice and it will always be your choice how you want to live.

It is one thing to realize that you are in a situation that has been created by guilt and shame. And it is another thing to see yourself as habitually choosing negative situations that creates more guilt and shame. Deciding to carry your past into your future does not mean you have to continue carrying it, either. It is a decision from the past, but that doesn't mean it has to look this way forever.

Our family value system is the pivot point of how we choose to relate to other people and have relationships. We may choose to marry, to stay single, to be interdependent on others or totally dependent emotionally on another as a direct result of our first seven years of programming, which we most likely are comfortable doing.

There may be consequences behind the choices of how we decide to show up and be a part of our relationship choices. Ultimately, we are the ones who decide what really works for us and what we need to let go of in order to grow and prosper in life. Now let's take a look at an example of how your family value system may impact your thinking and choices. Imagine you have a mother or father who tells you that you can never trust people. How easy would it be for you to trust another person? If you are raised in an alcoholic home, you learn to not trust yourself either. You are taught to suppress your true expression to avoid pain. So you protect your true self-expression. So, you may start a relationship built on false pretenses. Certainly not everyone lives this way, but if generations of individuals have this type of subconscious programming then are any of us living in our truth?

So, what we have created here is a duplication of our parents' value system that says that the man is the money maker and the woman is the homemaker. There is lots of evidence today to prove otherwise, but what about our programming and how that speaks to living in your truth?

What is missing here is the need for respect. Individuals need to feel respect from one another in order to feel valued.

So, I ask you to consider what your situation is right now. Is life what you always thought it would look like or is it made up of so many compromises that you have made or have you lost yourself?

Were you hanging on by a thread with your marriage because you did not feel you could start over again and questioning if you did if you would be successful?

If you were to fast forward your life to retirement is it what you expected it to look like? Do you wish you would have done things differently? Do you feel that you missed your calling?

Well, if you do it is not too late to make different choices in a new stage of your life.

Did your relationship grow through the years or did you feel that the struggles were sometimes not worth the effort you had to make to keep it going? When you create a solid foundation for yourself based in your truth if you want to you will attract a partner you will attract someone that compliments you. Correct? I am not trying to get you to question yourself as much as I want to get you to think about what it would feel like if you really felt fulfilled.

It is not a surprise if you answered by saying that you are thinking to yourself that you have not been as loyal to yourself as you would have liked to be. Everyone is entitled to take a closer look at their life choices without judgement and opt to reorganize their game plan and go forward with a new set of goals. If I didn't think that, I would have not written a book titled *Do I Need a Divorce to be Happy?*

You may not need to break your marriage to be happy. But you may need to break some long-time habits in your thinking. There is a specific process that you need to go through to understand your situation, and everyone's situation is different. I will guide you through that when it is time.

Chapter 7:

From Pain to Power

Let's talk a little bit about your definition of independence and dependence. How do you define them? What is your view on them if you put the word financial in front of them? Where do you see yourself and what does that look like for you? Take a moment to journal on your answers. How did you find that exercise?

Like I had mentioned in my personal story, there were major influences in my life that detoured the path to fulfillment and my true happiness.

Earlier I spoke about guilt. Guilt can wipe out our feeling of independence. In fact it is a useless emotion. It does not serve you or anyone else if you feel guilty. So, where does guilt come from? Guilt and shame are longtime emotional mindsets brought about by people who want to control their environment and the people in it. Guilt brings on shame if it is not processed to understand where it is coming from when you are feeling it. So why, you ask, would someone feel that making people feel guilty is the best way to motivate them? What would be the payoff for using this tactic? This type of mind-set blocks love from being at the center of the relationship because it is becomes fear driven. At this point I am referring to any type of relationship, be it personal or business, because it is unhealthy to function from a place of fear and it contaminates the relationship rather than feeding the relationship with the positive energy it needs to grow.

Now, I am going to suggest that you take out your journal again and jot down the following questions: Who am I? What do I want? And of course: What do I need to be happy? I must caution you that believing in miracles is a side effect of taking this journey within. If you are allergic to happiness you may find yourself running out to the drug store for Benadryl while you are reading this book.

Next, take a few cleansing breaths and ask yourself the following questions: How are you showing up in your life today? Are you wearing the clothes you want to wear and driving a car you want to drive, but still having dozens of thoughts running through your mind at the end of the day that are trying to tell you something is not right? I imagine the first thing that comes to mind is "I can't begin to entertain these questions with my life in the chaos that it is right now!" Chaos or doldrums, it may be time to take a mental health day and begin the process of re-evaluating your life circumstances.

Over the years, I have noticed that most people find it comforting to start the day with quiet time because once the day gets going it becomes more and more difficult to find the time to set goals for the day. At the end of the day, of course, most people will say that they are too tired to make time for themselves, but what I have found is that even taking a few minutes bringing awareness to what I accomplished during the day and then clearing my mind to set my intentions for the next day is quite helpful when it comes to manifesting my desired goals.

Actualizing the intentions you set for yourself and your goals can bring you a sense of joy. Another way to experience joy is to take a moment to acknowledge all that you have working for you in your life even if it is the smallest thing.

There is always an opportunity to experience gratitude at any given point during the day. The pathways in the brain are formed by habits. When the reward system is prompted by repetitive thoughts it creates a familiar feeling. These feelings are neither good nor bad. They are simply feelings that are familiar. This is how we train the brain and the pathways respond accordingly.

Now, if we start to examine the results we get from the habits we have formed, we will notice a common thread. Either we are motivated by fear or we are motivated by love. Love and fear are polar opposite emotions. Clearly, we are making choices every day about which side of the scale we decide to reside on, and upon examination, it becomes clear that we have a preference where we feel most comfortable. The glass will remain half-empty or half full until we decide to choose otherwise.

Chapter 8:

Set Yourself Free

The reality is that when you met your husband and decided to get married, your life goals and dreams were probably different than they are today. You have grown and changed from the time you met and the time you married. Your perspective on things may have also changed say from five years ago to ten years ago. Although you had dreams and goals for yourself, you also had them for your relationship and its future.

With regard to Melissa, she most certainly became a totally different person from the time she was planning to spend the rest of her life with John till now and that does not mean that their marriage is in trouble. It does show us though that they had to face a challenge and overcome it together. It also shows us the level of importance their marriage had become for them. They maintained the love and respect they have had for each other. When crisis hit their lives they were forced to discuss Melissa's dreams and goals and put her first. It was just as important for them to bring love and respect to discussing John's dreams and goals.

Love and trust are the essential ingredients in a relationship especially if we want it to be for the long term and they obviously have proven it to be true for them.

Alternatively, we can lose the love for our partner and the commitment for our relationship we once had when we fell in love with them. You're not alone, if this is your reality. It is common and it is actually a normal response to living in stressful circumstances with another person. Sometimes we find that we have aligned ourselves more with the goals and dreams of the other person's vision for our future rather than our own, similar to Melissa and John. This can result in a feeling of loss. Loss is painful and it needs to be honored. Without honoring the part of ourselves that needs our time and attention, we are partially alive. In order to live life fully it is important to collect our thoughts and feelings and honor them by journaling them and giving them the love and respect they deserve.

Life can feel like you are coming unglued at the core and then everything around it starts suffering due to a loss of control. If we become too caught up in chaos and crisis trying to keep everyone in our lives happy we lose our focus. Unfortunately, we cannot make others see our point of view nor should we expect them to change their point of view while we work hard at trying to convince them of our point of view. They may not want to hear what we are trying to tell them.

It has been said that love is a decision and conflict resolution means deciding to put aside our differences for the sake of the bigger picture and work toward a solution that benefits everyone. Now, I don't want you to walk away thinking that conflict resolves easily or that you will like being uncomfortable working through conflict, but consider the worst-case scenario if you don't address the problems when they come up. What will be the end result?

You could spend the rest of your life putting your energies into trying to get your husband to agree with you by fighting your reality day in and day out or turn, decide to choose a different way of approaching your life.

Chapter 9:

You Were Meant to Shine

By now you can see that the choice of what direction you head in is ultimately yours and making an attitude adjustment might be just what you need to accelerate the growth process, aligning you into seeing your vision of what you hope to achieve by working toward your goals and dreams to bring them to reality.

I suggest you take a moment to do this exercise. It will be a real eye-opening experience. Please take it seriously and make quiet time for yourself to take out your journal. At the top of the page, write the following: "the payoffs of staying stuck."

Try to recall all the reasons that make you feel so comfortable staying in an uncomfortable place in life and write in detail as much as you can expand upon what your decision is based on and then close your journal and walk away. Give yourself an opportunity to get a cup of tea and go back to your quiet space and read about your reasons to stay uncomfortable. How does it feel in your body to read what you wrote to yourself?

Did you find that your decision was based on the anticipated reactions you would get from your family and friends? A lot of people are afraid of making changes in their lives because they do not want the people to see them start making changes and then have them ask questions if they stopped and went back to their old ways.

Remember the bigger the rewards, the bigger the changes will need to be to get to those rewards. Expect that there will be strong reactions to the changes you begin making in your life. Don't let it distract you.

Now going back to how you view yourself stuck. What you don't have to face? What actions are you avoiding simply because you believe you don't have to do them? This is your comfort zone. What is the specific image you hold of yourself that you don't want anyone else to know about? Write all of this down in detail. After you finish journaling, take a moment to reflect on your answers. You will see the importance of this in the ten-step REINVENTED process.

Then, begin to explore the opportunities to be creative on any given day. Do you allow yourself the time to explore what you are capable of or have you closed yourself off for so long that you do not even know how to begin exploring? What is the image that comes to mind? Is it something you feel good about or would like to see it change? Once again, take out your journal and put some time into your answer. You may need to do a life review and list all of your accomplishments from present going backward to see how you recall the things you accomplished and forgot about. It is an interesting exercise and it triggers joyful memories. This can inspire you to try new things. Maybe you see other people doing things that you would like to try but are afraid of doing. Try it anyways.

These exercises are important because they help you to reconnect back to your feelings. If you are not in the habit of connecting to your feelings, it can be awkward in the beginning, but it can become resourceful for you.

You may find that thoughts and feelings you thought were no longer bothering you will surface and that writing about them can be healing. Review your journal once a week to review your progress and remind you of what you enjoy focusing on or concerns you want to release by putting them on paper instead of speaking about it with another person. Once you learn to appreciate the value of journaling you can begin to see your mind release its focus on your pain and it may give you a renewed sense of well-being.

Test out your experiences with journaling to get the most out of this personal care habit you have now created for yourself. You can have it work for you if you are patient enough to learn how to work with the skill set to find the best style to benefit your personal growth.

It is also a habit that can bring about your creative side and lead you to your artistic side by writing poetry or short stories. You can also use it as a tool for making changes happen in your life and working on decisions before putting them into action. You will have the benefit of seeing them on paper and creating different ways to approach your ideas then being able to review them before bringing them to life. You will also be able to get a bigger picture to see what makes the most sense to you before you decide to discuss it with someone.

When you make journaling a habit you will begin to notice that the quality of your communication with friends and relatives changes. You may feel that you are not as interested in gossip or comparing yourself so much to other people. These things only add to creating more confusion and take you off of focusing on clearing your mind so you can be open to better things entering your life.

Chapter 10:

Loving Lessons

S o, if you have had a taste of financial independence at one point in your life, do you find yourself desiring to have it again without breaking your marriage? After reading Melissa's story you may find the inspiration to do some soul searching.

Melissa and John's relationship had taken on its own life and the lesson they learned were about the importance of working together. Melissa learned that it did not serve her to continue repeating her co-dependent behaviors. John learned that being an absent partner did not serve him or his marriage. Looking back, we reviewed the definition of insanity and were reminded continuing to repeat old habits that do not serve you will keep you stuck. Ultimately, we learned the most important loving lesson and that is not to ignore your goals and dreams when they are tugging on your heartstrings. It does not matter how big or small they are they are important and so are your decisions.

Chapter 11:

Detachment

You learn many lessons by participating in twelve-step recovery groups. Primarily, you are taught the simplest way to reinforce the habit of having value for yourself is by being honest with yourself and others by identifying your boundaries. Boundaries were created in order to set limits. You need to have boundaries in your life to keep life simple and to protect yourself.

When you attend a CoDa meeting, which has been established for individuals struggling with codependency, detach with love. Detaching with love is a principle that not only is a boundary, but it helps to reinforce that you value yourself and the other person.

When you engage in negative behaviors and invite other people to participate in them with you, it makes your relationship toxic. When I refer to the term toxic, it is speaking to the part of the relationship that now has crossed over the line from a healthy relationship to an unhealthy way of behaving.

Learning healthy behaviors helps you maintain healthy relationships. Healthy relationships thrive and unhealthy relationships self-destruct. As you observed in Melissa's story, Melissa went from living her life with unhealthy behaviors to turning her life around, learning how to create healthy behaviors.

Melissa learned how to detach from John and her family with love in order to maintain her self-respect and it increased her self-esteem. She gained the respect of her husband and learned how to accept John's support.

Chapter 12:

Soaring

You will make more than one career change over your lifetime. I believe the average reported is that an individual will have ten career changes over a lifetime. The most valuable lesson that I have learned for myself and taught to others is the value of living in your own truth.

As I spoke about earlier, reflecting on the answers to your core value questions will lead you in the right direction in life. The point of reference I use here is that if you're living within your core values, your life will feel lighter. When you are living outside your core values, you will feel a sense of heaviness in your life.

I know you have accomplished a lot in your life so far and you know what works for you. Keeping a positive attitude, an attitude of gratitude and giving back to the world whatever way you choose will help keep the journey on the light side.

Believing in our goals and dreams, that we can have what we want, can be a risky proposition, but why deny yourself the opportunity of seeing your full potential manifest into reality?

Chapter 13:

Obstacles

In the previous chapters, I mentioned utilizing twelve-step recovery groups as the steps provide essential core values of learning how to live happy, joyous and free from emotional attachments that hold us back from living a healthy life. However, I recommend a healthy balance of professional counseling and twelve step recovery programming to work through issues of codependency.

The important thing is to not neglect your needs to be heard, supported, and acknowledged during any point in your life. Only people that judge help are the people that are afraid of it or tried it and doing the work scared them off.

I can go on and on for days about the fact that there will be obstacles that will come up. They will, and you will know how to overcome them because we have reviewed them and their purpose.

Let's talk a little bit about character building. What qualities do you think it takes to build good character? Take a moment to jot your thoughts down in your journal. They will serve as reinforcement and opportunity for review in the future.

Chances are if you are reading this book, you possess the gift of intuition. I applaud you for being willing to admit that. It is not easy for natural born leaders to admit that they need a little support, assistance, or counsel, but once given the opportunity they are like a fish that takes to water. They naturally help others and need to learn how to receive help as well as give help. It becomes the natural flow of yin and yang. Those that are not receptive to receiving help are doomed to repeat their past mistakes simply because they were too strong-willed to take that closer examination of self and make a couple adjustments.

It is human nature to not want to have to stop and examine the situation to see what simple adjustments would benefit the situation because of course, it may slow down the process of going forward, but isn't that the point of getting help?

Our thinking can get in the way of our best laid plans. Lite is too short to keep interfering with the universe's plans carefully, divinely laid out for us already. You need to know that all things have been predetermined long before you got here, mainly because you made choices ahead of time identifying what you want to accomplish in the short time that you are here on planet earth. I know sometimes it seems like forever, but that is usually when you are too young to drive, to drink, to be treated like an adult. God only knows as soon as we cross that threshold, time takes off like a rocket and we want to know why it is going so fast all the sudden. Our days and weeks go by and next thing you know the seasons are changing before we took the time to get to enjoy them.

Being natural born leaders, having the gift of intuition, we like the idea of being organized. It may not be our best quality, but we need to be organized in order to accomplish our goals and obtain what we want in life. We all have life lessons to learn and it is not always easy to be organized because we need to be able to take time to work with our gift of feeling and knowing how to incorporate this skill set into our success story.

I find it better to be organized and valuing your time and other's time during the day so that there is time to enjoy recreational activities. In my opinion, it is just a better way to live because life is more balanced this way.

So don't expect things to be perfect. Remember to ask for help when you need to and sometimes just ask anyways so you don't' forget to practice the value of asking.

Conclusion

Now that you have opened the door to the realm of possibilities for change, happiness, and growth, what will your decision be? Review the topics you have journaled on and take a moment to reflect on what you have learned about yourself and your point of view. See what you would like to expand on and what you realize it's time to eliminate making for the best version of yourself to be present in your life.

After reading this book, I hope that the answers that you were seeking became more clear. You may have found that things you were thinking about are starting to make a little more sense. This book offers you ten steps to the future you in the REINVENTED process. The specific steps of the REINVENTED process offers you are there as the guidelines I teach to building the confidence you desire to learn how to break free from financial codependency without breaking your marriage.

Remember, the only person who can truly stop you from your heart's desire is you. No one else has the power to get in your way unless you give them permission. If you have been giving your power away like Melissa was giving hers away, you may not have known how it happened and how to begin reclaiming your power.

Co-dependent behaviors are deeply rooted in the early stages of development in emotional and social development. Like all compulsive behaviors, as they are learned they can be unlearned by reprogramming your reward system with positive behaviors and incorporating a solid twelve-step recovery program.

I wrote this book in efforts to support and encourage all women who feel they have lost their sense of freedom and financial independence in their marriage.

Divorce does not have to be an option, so consider the possibilities of divorcing the current version of yourself and reconnecting to your relationship with a brand-new emerging version of yourself. I would like to refer to this version as the best version of yourself. Maybe one that you have dreamt about, but you were not clear on how to create.

Learn what you need to make yourself happy. Trust and believe that your wishes will be granted if your intentions are pure and not directed by self-will. Allow yourself to trust the process even if it means throwing up every time you move toward your goals and dreams. Trust me when I tell you it is worth every struggle to achieve your goals and dreams.

If your heart is screaming, "***Don't waste another day ignoring your goals and dreams,***" if you are feeling that you would like to achieve your goals and dreams faster with the author's help, you can reach out to me by email at beingpresent5@gmail.com

The universe is waiting for you to speak your truth and ready to assist you on your path to achieving your goals and dreams.

Remember you can do this. Enjoy the journey!

Thank You!

YOU WERE MEANT TO LIVE IN YOUR OWN TRUTH.

There is great power in reclaiming your ability to choose to live from your heart.

After reading this book if you say, "I'm ready to make the change I've always wanted to make, but I would like the author's help," then reach out to me at beingpresent5@gmail.com to schedule a FREE consult.

You can get an exclusive FREE BONUS CHAPTER never-before-published by signing up for my mailing list.

Consider what are you losing out on and what it is costing you to not solve this problem. What will your life look like and what will the consequences be for delaying the necessary action?

It's not just about giving yourself permission to nurture your heart's desire, but how taking action and believing in yourself will change your life. Consider what you are losing by not starting the process. Where will your goals and dreams end up?

About the Author

Teri Grayner has been working in the counseling profession for over eighteen years. She is most known for her inspirational spirit, holding her clients in high regard while providing counsel for them to work though their challenges in early recovery from the disease of addiction. She also knows what it takes to build a solid foundation to create a long-term recovery. Her practical approach, insight, and intuitive healing sensitivity make her unique in the counseling field. She holds a master's degree in professional counseling from Capella University and is a Licensed Alcohol and Drug Counselor. Her 10-Step Process of being REINVENTED is the working knowledge anyone seeking true success needs. She is advertised on the *Psychology Today* website and has a private practice in Ridgewood, NJ.